EVERYDAY CODING __

COMBINING TASKS

Using Composition

Elizabeth Schmermund

Cavendish
Square
New York

Published in 2018 by Cavendish Square Publishing, LLC
243 5th Avenue, Suite 136, New York, NY 10016

Copyright © 2018 by Cavendish Square Publishing, LLC

First Edition

Library of Congress Cataloging-in-Publication Data

Names: Schmermund, Elizabeth, author.
Title: Combining tasks: using composition / Elizabeth Schmermund.
Description: New York : Cavendish Square Publishing, 2018. | Series: Everyday coding
| Includes bibliographic references and index. | Audience: Grades 2-6.
Identifiers: ISBN 9781502632098 (library bound) | ISBN 9781502629807 (pbk.) |
ISBN 9781502629821 (6 pack) | ISBN 9781502629814 (ebook)
Subjects: LCSH: Computer programming--Juvenile literature. | Scratch (Computer program language)--Juvenile literature. | Programming languages (Electronic computers)--Juvenile literature.
Classification: LCC QA76.6 S36 2018 | DDC 005.1--dc23

Editorial Director: David McNamara
Editor: Caitlyn Miller
Copy Editor: Nathan Heidelberger
Associate Art Director: Amy Greenan
Designer: Christina Shults
Production Coordinator: Karol Szymczuk
Photo Research: J8 Media

Printed in the United States of America

TABLE OF CONTENTS __

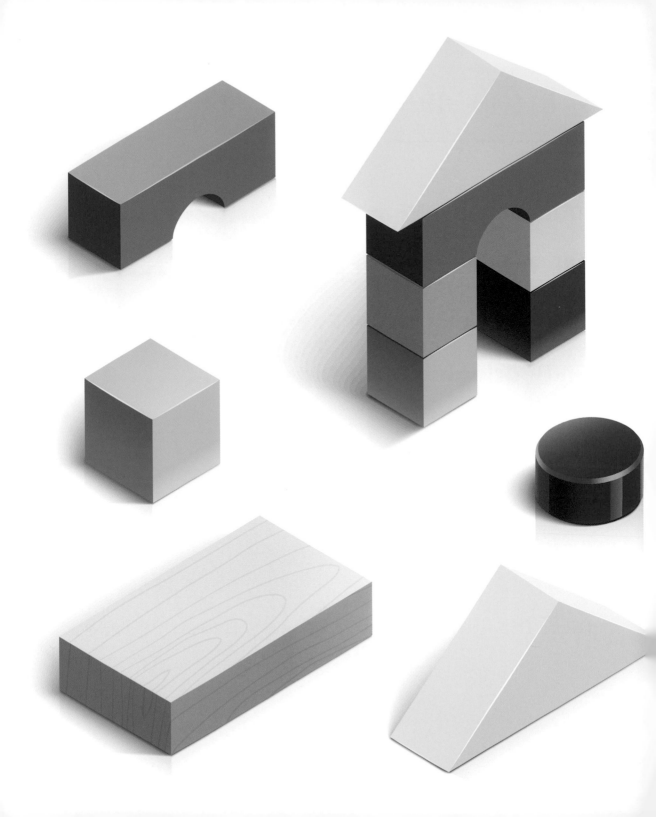

What Is Composition?

You've probably played with blocks at home or at school. You sit in front of a pile of them. You imagine what to build. Then you combine different pieces to bring your creation to life. Combining different pieces to build something new is called **composition**. You use composition all the time. In fact, you use it every day!

Opposite: Using composition is like building a block tower.

The word "composition" has many meanings. A composition can be a work of art. It can be a piece of literature or music. A recipe is composed of many ingredients. In coding, composition means something similar. It means combining different **tasks** into lines of **code**. Tasks need instructions. A computer must follow those instructions in order to do or create something.

Combining tasks helps **programmers**. Programmers use composition so they don't have to repeat lines of code. This means computer **programs** run faster. It also makes coding easier. Let's learn more about how we use composition.

CHAPTER 01

Taking a Closer Look

Have you heard a band play music? A band might have a drummer. There might be a guitar player. Many bands have a singer as well. Each person in the band plays or sings notes written just for them. Combining all their sounds makes a catchy song. This is a great example of composition.

Instead of playing a song, a programmer works to make a useful program. The programmer needs to add together different tasks. This makes

A band combines the sounds of different instruments.

Computers read code in the same way musicians read musical scores.

a **complex** program. Combining different tasks is how programmers do their job.

Imagine a programmer is making a game. In the game, players will collect coins. These coins earn points. A programmer does not need to write new code to add up a player's score for each level of the game. The programmer would use the same piece of "adding" code. She would

Games are made up of many parts. Each part has a lot of code behind it.

write the code once. Then she could add it into the code for a new level.

Programmers reuse pieces of code. They combine pieces of code to save time.

Programmers can combine code in other ways, too. A programmer combines code for sound effects, graphics, and buttons to click. These pieces are important parts of a game. Together they make the game fun. Adding pieces of code together is composition.

Think again about a band. Each band member plays his or her part. You can think about a song's different musical sections, too. Each of

Decomposition means taking something apart.

Decomposition

You can't talk about composition without talking about **decomposition**. Decomposition is the process of breaking down tasks. It is the opposite of composition. Remember that composition is combining different parts. Composition makes parts into a whole. Composition and decomposition are part of what is called **modularity**. Modularity means using smaller pieces of code in a smart way.

these sections has a set of instructions. Each musician must follow his or her instructions. You can change these instructions to make a new pattern. You can take some parts out. And you can add other parts in. This will create a whole new song. It might be completely different from the first one. It's different even though it contains many of the same "parts."

This is the same way coders work with code. A programmer can use an old piece of code in a brand new program. A programmer could use the "adding" code in the next game she makes. Programmers look for ways to save time. It would be silly to write new code if they've already done the work before.

CHAPTER 02

Composition in Everyday Life

Composition is something many artists use. Painters use different colors to make a picture. They also use different shapes. Composition is also something *we* use in everyday life. We might not even realize it. In some ways, the human mind works like a computer. Our minds—like computers—often work using modularity.

Opposite: When we draw, we are using composition.

Art, such as *The Starry Night* by Vincent van Gogh, is made up of colors, shapes, and more.

For example, think about getting ready for school. Getting ready involves multiple tasks or steps. These combine to reach the goal of getting to school on time. Think of one **module** as one task that will get us closer to our goal. An example is putting on clothes. The module of putting on clothes includes several different steps. All these steps must be combined together. Your steps might look like this:

- Select a shirt and pants

- Put on a shirt and pants

- Put on socks

- Put on shoes

We can arrange these steps in different orders. However, some steps must be done in

Tying your shoes is an example of a module.

a certain order. You can put jeans on first or your shirt on first. But you have to put on socks before shoes!

All of us think in this way. It is a modular way of thinking. We break down problems into different steps. We tackle these steps in different ways. However, we must also recombine these steps together to reach our ultimate goal. This is composition in action.

Modularity is like a puzzle where all the pieces fit with every other piece.

Puzzle Pieces

You can think of modularity as a puzzle composed of different puzzle pieces. However, this is a special puzzle. Its pieces all fit together with every other piece. They can be arranged in different ways. The pieces do not change at all. Yet the way in which they are arranged will change the color and shape of the puzzle as a whole. This is how coders use modularity to build programs.

To cook, you need to add together ingredients.

Let's take a look at another example. Imagine that you want to make pancakes. To do so, you need to take out all of the ingredients. Then, you need to place them on the counter. You'll need milk, eggs, butter, sugar, flour, salt, and baking powder. Think of each of these ingredients as a module. Each has its own set of instructions. For

Each ingredient is important to the composition: breakfast!

example, you beat the eggs. You also melt the butter. We combine all of these different modules together into a bowl.

Sometimes the order of the steps matters. That's like when you mix together wet ingredients first. Other times, the order doesn't matter. In combining all these ingredients together, we

Eating a delicious breakfast that you've made is like writing a great program.

reach our goal. The ingredients are like modules. Eating a delicious breakfast of fluffy pancakes is like writing a great program.

```
closest",a)},index:function(a){ if ( a
parentNode)&&a.nodeType!==11?a null},parents:function(a){
ibling(a.parentNode.firstChild,a)},children:function(a){
b,d){if(d)a=":not("+a+")";return b.length===1 c.find
embed|hr|img|input|link|meta param)((([\w:]+)[>]|)[^>]
"<map>","</map>"],_default:[0,"",""]};P.optgroup P.option
his[0]){var b=c(a,this[0].ownerDocument).eq(0).clone
n(){return this.parent().each(function(){c.nodeName
length){var a=c(arguments[0]);a.push.apply(a,this.toArray
yTagName("*"));c.cleanData([e])}e.parentNode e.parentNode
.replace($,"")],e)[0]}else return this.cloneNode(true)
TML=a}}catch(e){this.empty().append(a)}} c.isFunction(a)
,detach:function(a){ return this.remove(a,true)},
gment;if(f=h.childNodes.length===1 h h.firstChild h.first
ckClone||!Da.test(a[0]))){f=true; (h c.fragments[d])
var h=d.length;f<h;f++){var l=(f 0 this.clone(true)
x=o[0],r=b.createElement("div"); for (r.innerHTML o[] l
(e&&c.nodeName(f[h],"script")){ f[h].type
```

CHAPTER 03

Bringing It All Together

Anything you can think of is made of smaller parts. To write a story, you put together words. These words form sentences. You combine sentences. Now you have paragraphs. Code is the same. Lines of code can be combined together into modules. Those modules are combined into programs. Composition is an important part of every program. That's because

Opposite: Lines of code are combined to make programs.

modularity is a way to think about programming. Remember that modules are pieces of a program. Modules complete a task.

Programmers can break down tasks into smaller modules. This is decomposition. Then they recombine these modules. Programmers do this to accomplish new, bigger tasks. This is composition. Many programs are made of bits and pieces of other programs. Those pieces have been recycled. Different modules are pieced together. Now they work together in new ways.

Many programmers recycle old code in new programs.

Getting a computer to draw a circle is a complex task.

Let's say you want to get your computer to perform a task. You want the computer to draw a circle. This task might seem very simple. Actually, it involves several steps. First, a computer must know *where* to draw a circle on the screen. Next, you need to tell the computer *how large* the circle should be. You'll need to make many other decisions.

What color will the circle be? How thick will the circle be? Will it change colors? You will need

A computer can draw a more complex circle, like Earth. That just requires more modules combined together.

to write at least three sets of instructions, or modules. These modules answer the graphics questions you thought about. Most likely, you will need many more sets of instructions. It can require quite a few lines of code to get a computer to draw a circle!

This is where composition comes in. Composition helps programmers make a task like drawing a circle easier. It also makes that code simpler. A programmer could call her composed instructions for drawing a circle "drawCircle."

Scratch's mascot
is Scratch the Cat.

Scratch: Coding for Kids

Scratch is a **programming language**. It was developed by the Massachussets Institute of Technology (MIT) Media Lab. Scratch is a great way to learn coding. You can use it to create animations and games. It is also a fun way to experience composition. "Scratching" means reusing and remixing code. You can start experimenting with Scratch coding at https://scratch.mit.edu.

Part of learning to code is learning to think about all of the tasks you want to combine.

The computer will know what the command "drawCircle" means. It means that it needs to perform all the different tasks involved. Then it will fulfill this basic command. The programmer has also **condensed** many lines of code. Now all that code is one simple command. Both the

Any time you see code, look for composition!

computer and other programmers will know what "drawCircle" does.

This programmer has successfully made her own composition. She will now be able to use this code in future programs. Composition makes hard tasks easy!

code Instructions that direct a computer to carry out certain tasks.

complex Something with many pieces.

composition In programming, composition is combining pieces of code or modules to complete a task. These combinations make programming easier.

condensed To have made something shorter or simpler.

decomposition The process of breaking something down.

modularity Decomposing computer programs or codes into smaller parts and then recomposing and reusing those parts in different ways.

module A part of a program or code that contains one or more tasks for a computer to carry out.

program A set of instructions telling a computer what to do.

programmer Someone who writes computer programs, or instructions to make a computer carry out certain tasks.

programming languages A language that is used to communicate instructions to a computer.

Scratch A free programming language that helps kids learn to code.

task A piece of work to be done.

Books

Wainewright, Max. *Code Your Own Games!: 20 Games to Create with Scratch*. New York: Sterling Children's Books, 2017.

Woodcock, John. *Coding Games in Scratch*. New York: DK Kids, 2015.

Websites

Computer Science Unplugged

http://csunplugged.org

Discover more about computer science.

Scratch

https://scratch.mit.edu

Learn to code in this visual programming language.

INDEX

Page numbers in **boldface** are illustrations.

Elizabeth Schmermund is a writer, scholar, and editor. She lives in New York with her family. Elizabeth enjoys writing books for students of all ages. She hasn't yet developed her own computer programs. However, she uses composition every day to write!